MERCENARY ENGLISH
Second Edition

Mercedes Eng

Mercenary Press

MERCENARY ENGLISH
Mercedes Eng

Copyright © 2016
Second edition, first printing

Published by Mercenary Press
www.mercenaryenglish.com
innercitykitty604@gmail.com

Cover and interior images by Gord Hill
Typesetting by Andrea Actis and Danielle LaFrance

Eng, Mercedes
    Mercenary English / Mercedes Eng.

Poems.
ISBN 978-0-9958090-0-0

Cataloguing information for this book is available from the Library and
Archives Canada | www.collectionscanada.gc.gc

for Terrylynn Rivard McDonald

address to the city

project civil city i call you out
reduce homelessness by half?
half measure don't do for this half breed
most livable city i call you out
jamie graham, jim chu i call you out
anne drennan, catherine galliford
former police and rcmp spokespersons
for your complicity while living in a
woman's body
i call you out women
i call all you motherfuckers out

every
single
one
of
you
who looked away
while women were murdered
left right and centre
in this dream city
this gold mountain city
with its cold coal heart

i call you out

Contents

KNUCKLE SANDWICH

lawyer said
serial killer suffered
a miscarriage of justice

let the women carry this miscarriage of justice on their backs

let them give birth to this miscarriage of justice

The Highway of Tears

what caused the tears?

who caused whose tears?

what about the tears?

those deep structural tears in the warm blanket of our multicultural nation

unseen until

until

"the victims, female prostitutes"

until

"high-risk lifestyle"

until

"the city's gritty Downtown Eastside"

until

"serial killer"

until

Jack the Ripper

until

social anomaly takes blame

until

"butchered remains"

"butchered their bodies"

until

"slaughterhouse"

until

the abattoir enters your boudoir

Vancouver authorities recorded a sharp increase in attacks
made by styling tools—a situation putting more and more
Vancouverites ill at ease

unseen until

until

profit by war machine

and seen

When the media do focus on violence against women of colour, they most often invoke the banner of culture to explain such violence. This is a culturalization of violence and culture becomes the framework used by white society to pre-empt both racism and sexism.

The increasingly alarming state of affairs has reached an all-time high as women from Vancouver reported more and more attacks by hairdryers.

"The veil commands me to take my hands off my hips, round my shoulders, and lower my chin."

does it now?

but that's not our problem

our problem is Pickton

(was Gilbert Paul Jordan)

(was...)

and dealt with

we washed our hands

done

in the past

just like those vanishing Indians

The Murdered and Missing Women 2.0

"The burqa tells the world, 'Do not acknowledge I am here.' But it is also a message for the woman who wears it: You are entitled to just this much physical space."

does it now?

the cowboys and indians
master narrative
has been directly implicated as contributing to the killing
of other dark-skinned people in other parts of the world
who have been regarded as impediments to American colonial
progress

Ever since the young woman with shiny jet-black hair has used a hair treatment by a brand we are unable to mention here, the attacks appear to have quite simply come to a stop.

somebody fly a jet

into this black mass of towers

that is her hair

and shines like justice

otherwise you might get tangled up in it

blinded by its shine

The visibility accorded to one expression or manifestation of violence and the invisibility of the other are interlocked. One supports and depends upon the other.

please read the charges

number of missing and murdered aboriginal women in Canada

number of Canadian soldiers killed in Afghanistan

number of Afghan women killed during Canada's leadership role
in the war

hey

let's make a sandwich

you guys can be the meat

who is the bread

collective womb

prairie bread basket

Ceres

who feeds all

(the right) children

she is capital eye

Islam has become the culturalist explanation for a variety of
different ills including
the subordination of women and the emerging terrorist threat
within the homeland. This trope persists because it is easy, accessible,
iconic, resonant with the historical context of Orientalism,

and ultimately a powerful strategic tool

There was a cowboy, an Indian, and a Muslim standing at
the edge of the world. The Indian said my people were once
great in number but now are few. The Muslim said my people
were once small in number and now are great. The cowboy said
that's because we haven't played cowboys and Muslims yet.

sometimes I wanna wear a hijab when white men reach out to stroke my shiny jet-black hair

sometimes I want that "invisibility" white female journalists seem to know so much about

Among the unfortunate victims, a disturbing pattern has emerged: damage inflicted by the attacker includes damaged, ravaged and sometimes even burnt hair.

until hair like amber waves of grain

New Highway of Heroes signs have been installed along the route,
commemorating Canadian soldiers
who have made the surpreme sacrifice in the line of duty.
The 172-kilometre stretch of Highway 401 will keep its official name,
the Macdonald-Cartier Freeway

should she keep the official name you gave her?

*The visibility accorded to one expression or manifestation of
violence and the invisibility of the other are interlocked.
One supports and depends upon the other.*

she

Cpl. Catherine Galliford, RCMP Missing Women Spokesperson
says: the first thing
we would like to say
is that we apologize to the families of the missing women
involved in our investigation. A leak of information to the news
media today, from an unknown source, created a situation in which
many family members were suddenly being contacted
without first getting the facts from the police.

investigation

information

first

families

first

facts

says: some of the activities on that property included the raising and slaughtering of animals, including pigs. Our continuing investigation has yielded information that meat products from the farm may have been obtained by

says: human DNA

The binary construction of the Muslim Woman, a construction that corrals religion and cultural practices as pillars upholding the faulty logic of the West, this binary posits that a Muslim woman can only be two things, either uncovered, and therefore

liberated,

or veiled, and thus still to some degree,

subordinated.

just how you want it
you wanna do the liberating
you don't want that
sweet little piece of dark meat
unwrapped

where's the fun in that?
the mystery
the dance
the tearing of a 1000 veils

hey

let's make a sandwich

a hero sandwich

rescuer
victim
victimizer

Thousands of motorcyclists took to the Trans-Canada Highway on Saturday to show support for Canadian soldiers killed in Afghanistan.

now that's progress

from a

Trail of Tears

to a

Highway of Tears

Motorcyclist wants to see the creation of a Highway of Heroes dedicated to fallen B.C. soldiers similar to the one in Ontario: It would be nice to have one out here 'cause it's not just soldiers from Ontario, it's soldiers from across Canada...we lose soldiers from across this great nation of ours so to have one out here would be amazing.

the Native Women's Association of Canada has documented

over 500 cases of Aboriginal missing and murdered women

from Vancouver's Downtown Eastside (and Prince George and

Edmonton and...) and across Canada over the last 30 years

I'm tripping on fallen soldiers all over the goddamn place

she

Det. Cst. Sheila Sullivan, Vancouver Police Missing Women Spokesperson
says: we are asking anyone who still has in their possession
any meat obtained from the farm to immediately
contact the Missing Women Task Force.

says: our chief reason for having people contact us is that the
meat in their possession, the meat obtained from the farm,
may have been exposed to, or is possibly connected to, existing
evidence that is related to the murder charges against Mr.
Pickton.

murder doesn't taste so good

now that you good citizens might have eaten some of it

Victims break through the pain and speak out. 'I wanted to break our silence,' was Valery B's spontaneous answer when asked by our special correspondent why she was speaking out now. 'It's unbelievably hard for me to talk about, especially when most people don't take it seriously. But looking after the health of your hair is far from superficial.'

it's deadly serious

Pat Robertson: Our CBN News war correspondent Paul Strand is embedded with the army's mechanized Third Infantry Division. He's travelling along with them. And Paul, can you tell us approximately where you are?

Paul Strand: We're, I would say, dozens of miles from Baghdad. I just talked to our commander, and he asked that I not be too specific about direction or distance; I think you can understand that. So far, everywhere we've gone we have seen artillery ahead of us and then artillery behind, and we're getting reports that there's fighting in all of the cities we've been through. So, I guess if this were the Old West, I'd say that there are Injuns ahead of us, Injuns behind us, and Injuns on both sides too.

"The fact that Bin Laden had been killed by US Special Forces was reported to President Obama on Sunday with the words, 'Geronimo EKIA.'"

B.C.'s inquiry into the death and disappearance of

women from Vancouver's Downtown Eastside

opened amid the chants of protesters

Commissioner Wally Oppal opened the inquiry by saying a key question he wants
answered at the inquiry is whether
society's most vulnerable women
are being treated the same as other citizens by the police and the law

m   i   s   s   i   n   g

from the inquiry
are more than a dozen non-profit advocacy groups
that were granted standing but withdrew because they were
denied public legal funding

Independent lawyer Robyn Gervais, who was appointed by Oppal
to represent the interests of aboriginal people,
resigned last month
amid complaints
that the inquiry was not focusing enough on

the native women who were among the victims

The visibility accorded to one expression or manifestation of
violence and the invisibility of the other are interlocked.
One supports and depends upon the other.

A proposed class action against the RCMP, alleging widespread
mistreatment of female officers of the police force, will be filed in
B.C. Supreme Court

at the missing inquiry

Galliford, once an RCMP spokeswoman

in the high-profile Air India case and the Missing Women Task Force,

claimed she was repeatedly sexually harassed by RCMP officers

"Galliford said, 'tell the women's families I've got their backs.'"

FEBRUARY 2010

I'm standin next to a mountain
and I chop it down with the edge of my hand

—Jimi Hendrix

"Harriet Nahanee jailed for protesting Sea to Sky Hwy. No medical
care; died of pneumonia. #Olympics are on #unceded Native #land.
pls. rt"

—*ungag me* paper dolls project

....

chopped a mountain down

my woman holds me down

my women hold me down

February 14th 2010

today when I represent
I think I'll need to dress carefully
thick socks heavy shoes jeans long sleeves
if I get smooshed into the pavement
maybe the clothes'll help
"the whole world will be watching"
so why do I feel like I need armour
in order to represent my sisters?
I don't know why I'm more scared of the Man in public
than I ever was of a strange man in an industrial park
is it because then I had a man's dick in my mouth
but now I wanna use my mouth to speak to the Man,
and He and I both know how powerful that is?

then they came

/ / / / / / / \ \ \ \ \ \ \ \ \ \ \ / / / / / / / / / / / / \ \ \ \ \ \ \ \ \
\ \ \ \ \ \ \ \ / / / / / / / / / / / \ \ \ \ \ \ \ \ \ \ / / / / / / / / / / /
/ / / / / / / \ \ \ \ \ / / / / / / / \ \ \ \ \ / / / / / / / \ \ \ \ \ \ / / / /

a friend in response to my amazement over the surveillance,
especially where I live downtown:

"you're in Fort Knox"

What's the gold?

....

"what I did on my summer vacation"

My dad wouldn't let me watch the torch relay with my school today;
my mom says it's important but my dad says there's YouTube.

They kept selling out but my mom made sure I had the red mittens to
wear as I waved at the cameras at the torch relay today.

I got in trouble for peeing my pants because we waited so long for the
torch to come and I had to go and I couldn't hold it but my dad said
we're not missing Canadian history goddamn it Craig!

I watched my mom, aunties, and elders interrupt the torch relay today.
Twice.

When you become a police officer, people trust you with their property and with their lives. Law enforcement is more than just a job—it's a calling. Is police school calling you?

it's calling someone

/ /

"Later in the morning, Constable Peters recalled Constable Kojima making the comment, 'now that was the shit you signed up for.'"

don't hate on me
because
i can't find my voice
you with your 6 foot whatever inches
your 200 and whatever pound frame
your history of activism
don't call me out
cause I'm just getting started
you with your "you think you're special cause you're an artist" shit
who do you think you're talking to?
don't discount
my time
on the frontlines
i didn't' speak then either
mouth to full to spit my anger out

my voice
it's mine to find
when it comes
my call will make you deaf

1 step forward, 2 steps back

....

opening my mouth to shut it

....

did you make any money? i didn't make any money.

a few days ago
my voice reverberated off the concrete walls
of old and new buildings that surround tentcity
when I spit my rhymes
for the Downtown Eastside

a weekend is week is a month
and i open it to say
our workshirt is mended

he says / he yells / he is confounded

"let's get em!"
—old white man watching protesters break windows of
the Canadian institution that broke backs and wombs
of brown-skinned women

\ \

divisiveness
multiple points of penetration
but only one fence and which side you standin on

dialogue at the throw down

hey white boy, you
with your smash the state no time for talking agenda
trying to tell me words are meaningless inaction
I didn't realize that
coloured-female-15-grand-a-year-in-wages me doesn't
fit your
anti-capitalist anti-colonialist anti-oppression work

there are different frontlines

my first one was home
then low track
then off to suck another kind of dick
the $8 an hour kind

now I spend my time at the university
and it ain't no frontline
and I don't feel real
cause most of the people around me aren't
and I want comrades not a cohort

then again
there's my professors marching like you
but yeah, fuck those upper-middle class white guys
let's talk about me

remember that where you came from
is different from me
when you say
my words
don't mean shit
cause they don't constitute
action

they made concrete tremble

....

she's a hundred fucking feet tall, my woman with feet on the ground

....

J'accuse   I am humbled
J'accuse   I am humbled
J'accuse   I am humbled

....

violence: the exercise of physical force so as to inflict injury on,
or cause damage to, persons or property; action or conduct
characterized by this; treatment or usage tending to cause bodily
injury or forcibly interfering with personal freedom

words are confusing
is "property damage" violence?
are "persons" and "property" the same thing?
what's the one for the big men dressed in boots and helmets,
holding shields, holding assault rifles?

goddamn, i want an assault rifle

under the stars and the surveillance

red tents on top of red brick poetry in the street

i

    lost

       time

              it flew away

          caught

         swirled up

into the vortex of helicopter propellers that pervaded dreaming

    eaten up

        spit out

scattered on the ground

everything was different and the same

....

do you hear me yet?

me: so i was with this trick outside the sugar refinery and—

you: wait, like the bar, or like the processing factory?

me: yeah, the actual refinery. so anyways…

"Cash for Cops"

U.S. government funds **$1 BILLION** to hire new police

Earn your Degree and become a hero!

Become a...

*Police Officer

*Crime Scene Investigator

*Federal Agent

hey. that happened here too.

••

my women hold me down

with their bones in the ground
with their bodies bound
with their voices hushed of sound
my women hold me down

the helicopters are gone
and with them our revolution sex
as your baton marks
fade
from this body
and the sonics of surveillance
from this head
so to
does
our revolution romance

it can't be captured by your closed-circuit cameras

a conversation with two young officers at a friend's apartment
on gold medal hockey/closing ceremonies night in the heart of
Robson red bloc headquarters

I hear steps behind me as I enter the lobby and turn around
to see who wasn't buzzed in
one smiles, says

don't worry, you can trust us

I look right into his boyish, handsome face
and then the other one's and I say

no, I don't think so

he smiles at his buddy, replies

ouch! ...stone cold

did the cops just flirt with me?

you shut your mouth
or I'll shut it for you

....

....

you talk about rupture

I talk about suspension

we talk about rupture

we talk about suspension

she says you talk about space

she says I talk about time

Vancouver police have a new crowd control device capable of emitting painfully loud blasts of sound, just in time for the 2010 Winter Olympics, CBC news has learned.

The medium-range acoustic device (MRAD) can use sound as a weapon, emitting piercing sounds at frequency levels that cross the human threshold of pain and are potentially damaging to hearing, say audio experts

short range poetic device

The pirate radio signal, 91.5 FM, that began
streaming from VIVO Media Arts on the eve of the
Lunar New Year, has been shut down by Industry
Canada after less than 24 hours of broadcast time.

"They gave us the standard line," said a spokesperson
for Soundscapes Co-op Radio, explaining that the
Industry Canada officers arrived in Olympics clothing.
"Proximity of the FM band to air traffic…we must
verify that the signal is consistent and not impinging
on another signal."

you hush your mouth missy!

Vancouver 2010 Winter Wardrobe

$200 marc jacobs protest purse, its turquoise Italian leather
ruined/renderedmoreauthenticallyrevolutionary
by Vancouver Media Coop sticker
thought it was a good choice
small and unobstrusive in a crush

$200 earnest sewn jeans
oily like the found wood that burns in the fires at tent city
good for sitting on the crushed brick the pavement the mud

workshirt, my man shirt, my protection
ok, it's a vintage 80s ralph lauren oxford shirt
$5 at Mintage

$350 club monaco trick-bought black wool coat
built to last, just like my back
it served me well and kept me warm when others weren't
and then it served me well and kept me warm when others weren't
and when I couldn't get warm on the inside, bourbon

$39.99 club monaco burgundy wool newsboy cap
didn't quite keep my head from flying off my shoulders

$16.99 h&m brass knuckles
holding me to the ground
allowing me to make sound

an arsenal of poems in my pocket

words like judgmental, melodramatic, teenager, mine

....

Does The Forgotten add to the body of contentious representation through its reproduction of stereotypical imagery that portrays the women as criminals and isolated victims without families or loved ones?

For example, you say you've changed the scale of the images in order to disallow viewers to look away, in contradistinction to the reward poster, which presents images of the women in a grid so that it is difficult to view the women as individuals. How do you redirect our gaze while using the same photographs as the basis of your work?

What is the difficulty, if any, of using these inscribed images of the women that correspond to the public's perception of them?

What alternative narrative of the women's lived experiences do your portraits seek to tell? What story do you tell with Mona Wilson's portrait, for example, which incorporates text, and stitched-up cuts and tears to the canvas?

How does your experience as a model—as an object of the gaze, rather than as the creator of the object to be looked at—inflect your work? Can you talk about what it's like to move back and forth between those two subject positions? What is this experience like in your performative work, where you occupy both positions at once, as creator of the work and as part of the work, since your being watched is part of the art itself?

Why were you being filmed during the 2010 Women's Memorial March?

Who the fuck do you think you are?

the eagles know

AUTOCARTOGRAPHY

PRINCE RUPERT

BRITISH
COLUMBIA

NORTHERN GATEWAY
1:100,000

EXXON
VALDEZ

G. HILL · 2012

Literally meaning the science or practice of map-drawing, cartography is integral to the exercise of colonial and neo-colonial power. The products of precise research, the first physically accurate maps were constructed in the early Modern period with the development of navigational aids and effective mapping tools. The cartography that followed in the seventeenth and eighteenth centuries paved the way for nineteenth century expansion.

initially created for

mercenary pursuits

maps marked out

trade routes between Europe and the trading posts of the East

benefiting merchants who called for new accurate maps

I call for new accurate maps

how it is (November 2007)

MAIN	MAIN
Owl Drugs	the heart of the community
no-name money mart	the Roosevelt
Hotel Washington	Coastal Health Authority
convenience store	the Regent
empty building	closed business
the Balmoral	closed business
pizza shop	closed business
porn store	closed business
Insite (North America's 1st legal safe injection site)	the Blue Eagle
Vancouver Drug School	the Brandiz
empty lot	closed business
empty building (the old Smilin' Buddha where my dad saw Jimi Hendrix)	convenience store
	convenience store
art gallery	
	COLUMBIA
subsidized housing project	
	Pigeon Park Savings
COLUMBIA	
	empty lot
pawn shop	
	convenience store

empty building development

parking lot

United We Can
(poor people endeavouring every day
to make money by cleaning up your
environmentally friendly water bottles)

ginseng store

the Dodson

drop-in for the street

meth clinic

art gallery

CARRALL

Pigeon Park

pawn shop

closed business

the Backpacker's Inn

Army and Navy

closed business

closed hotel

Funky Winkerbean's

the Shaldon

meth clinic

subsidized housing project

closed business

the Only

subsidized housing project

Downtown Eastside Residents Assc.
(they helped my dad then me with housing)

empty building development

CARRALL

Contemporary Centre for Asian Art

subsidized housing project

closed business

pawn shop

BladeRunners

empty lot

closed business

the Grand Union

subsidized housing project

Save-On-Meats	ABBOTT
pawn shop	closed pawn shop
empty building development	convenience store
hooker store (Model Express)	Salvation Army drop-in
empty lot	the Golden Crown
ABBOTT	closed business
Woodward's development	closed business
store selling Chinese stuff	closed business
Money Mart	the Triple Crown
CAMBIE	discount fabric store
	empty heritage building
	CAMBIE

low track

it's twelve midnight
and the hustle begins
eastside hustle, nobody wins
kitty's gonna bounce to the track
kitty's gonna skip to that trick
lean on the car door, have a chat
let him think he's brought the mac
be a bit sassy
so the cake'll lead him back
and for a little price
kitty's got her smack

cause once she catches that mark
kitty's gonna light the spark
then it's bang bang bang
till mr. trick hits his mark
a lil stack, made on her back

kitty's gonna jump off the stroll
to where the boys and girls go
lookin for the dope to fill the hole

so they're off to by the hour rooms
where kitty done seen so many moons
this man, he wants it unwrapped
cause he can tell by lookin
she's unclapped
but to kitty that's a no
a please and an extra twenty
don't make it a go
okay now man you down to the wire
cock that four four and fire

kitty's got three more
beatin beatin on her door
kitty's gonna jump off the stroll
to where the boys and girls go
lookin, lookin, lookin

then it's back to the corner to troll
and kitty hooks another
this one she knows well
lawyer from the westside
he asks her, yeah he tells her
why don't you quit that smack
but keep openin those legs
that way you still got the money
without lookin like you're running low on honey

enough talk woodsman
grind that axe
cause your time
it's at the max

kitty's gonna jump off the stroll
to where the boys and girls go
lookin, lookin, never findin

this one, he wanna go twice
second time half price
but kitty learned capitalism well
she knows time is money
gotta bring many bees to her honey
second time takes a long time
and she's workin for little
but she ain't workin for a dime

so kitty's gonna jump off the stroll
go pick up, go fix up
go fall down that hole

schoolyard hooker

another day another dollar
i'm standin on my corner
and who do i see
but a lil babygirl
from the same lil town as me

i know her from back in the day
when our daddies robbed we would play

she's only five feet
narrow as a side street
and lookin, lookin
like she did when we were innocent
when we didn't open our legs to pay rent

i ask after her mom and dad
and do they know
she's on the stroll
they know how it is,
she tells me

her daddy sure knows
cause next time i see her
she's buyin him a rock
and he knows she got the cash suckin cock

well natasha, she's gotta eat
girl's out on the street
making money to eat

she's barely five feet tall
you push her she falls
tasha, she's been workin since she was 13
went to what our daddies called school of hard knocks
but for you old men, it wasn't about hard cocks

even though we standin here
sellin our wares
like we ain't got cares
and though we both been tired for years
it moves me to tears

that this is the same lil girl
i used to run the block with

still runnin, but a different block now
this one no play time no pickup sticks
this one sell time pick up tricks
and tasha she picks up quick
the ones who like em young
she does the trick

tasha's daddy is conspirin in a murder plot
feedin off her while she's still hot
but like other girls on the stroll, she's fadin
a lot less customers and a whole lotta waitin

and soon that bad daddy of hers will be gone

global hooker

the way she told it
it was like the wild west
men cussin, fightin, put to the test
gals all sassy, can drink with the best
makin that money, fuck all the rest

the way she told it
it was summer vacation
goin to hawaii for a weekend trip
no need to pack, he'll buy all that
first class flight
fancy cocktails all night
but too many showers
hot water for hours
and your skin gets dry
but you don't cry
cause you're movin
cause you're shakin
bringing home that bacon

the way she told it
it was studio 54 in a snowglobe
when she disrobe
boys be cryin, men be vyin
wanna be havin, wanna be buyin

the way she told it
it was like carnival
hot sand, hotter sun
good food, better rum
the shimmy shake
always on the take
always on the make
the way she told it

blue skyes hooker

on the corner
she's trying
in the street
she's crying
but on pop rocks
she's flying

so if she's trying but failing

so if her man is lying, if he's denying
but the men are eyeing, still buying
then it's time for Skye to take flight

but babygirl didn't know you couldn't just up and run into a name
something she tried to do when mindflight wasn't enough

just up and running down the hallway and up out the window
trying to fly into that blue she named herself after

how it is (June 2009)

MAIN	MAIN
Owl Drugs	the heart of the community
no-name money mart	the Roosevelt
Hotel Washington	Coastal Health Authority
convenience store	the Regent
empty building	closed business
the Balmoral	closed business
pizza shop	closed business
porn store	closed business
Insite (North America's 1st legal safe injection site)	the Blue Eagle
art gallery	the Brandiz
community garden	art gallery
empty building (the old Smilin' Buddha where my dad saw Jimi Hendrix)	convenience store
	convenience store
art gallery	
	COLUMBIA
subsidized housing project	
	Pigeon Park Savings
COLUMBIA	
	empty lot
pawn shop	
	convenience store
huge housing development	

huge housing development continued

United We Can
(poor people endeavouring every day
to make money by cleaning up your
environmentally friendly water bottles)

ginseng store

the Dodson

drop-in for the street

meth clinic

art gallery

CARRALL

Pigeon Park

pawn shop

closed business

the Beacon Hotel

Army and Navy

Vancouver Women's Health Collective

empty building

Funky Winkerbean's

Save-On-Meats minus the meat

the Shaldon

meth clinic

subsidized housing project

closed business

the Only, closed due to the Health Act
(I never got sick eating there)

subsidized housing project

Downtown Eastside Residents Assc.
(they helped my dad then me with housing)

the Pennsylvania Hotel

CARRALL

Contemporary Centre for Asian Art

empty hotel: dev. app. no. DE411818

Pot Luck Café

empty lot

empty lot

empty lot

empty lot

the Grand Union

subsidized housing project

the unbuilt second half of a planned condo dev.

the first and built part of that development

hooker store (Model Express)

empty lot

ABBOTT

Woodward's development

store selling Chinese stuff

art gallery

fancy furniture store

retail space for lease

CAMBIE

ABBOTT

closed pawn shop

convenience store

Salvation Army drop-in

the Golden Crown

retail space in development

retail space in development

retail space in development

retail space in development

discount fabric store

Vancouver Film School

CAMBIE

representation of hooker

i am not a dismembered head with
a pair of hands inside it
i am not dna evidence on a farm
i am not a mugshot
i am not a pair of legs for you to
look at and buy
i am not a subject/object of your intellectual discourse
i am not a future you fear for your
wayward teenage daughters

i breathe
i shout
and
i get mad

someone told me
my anger is a gift
and
I'm gonna knock your teeth out with this gift.

how it is (January 2012)

MAIN	MAIN
Owl Drugs	the heart of the community
no-name money mart	the Roosevelt
Hotel Washington	rest in peace AM & VS
convenience store	the Regent
empty building	dev. app. no. DE414810
the Balmoral	dev. app. no. DE414810
pizza shop	dev. app. no. DE414810
porn store	dev. app. no. DE414810
Insite	dev. app. no. DE414810
art gallery	the Brandiz
community garden	art gallery
empty building (the old Smilin' Buddha where my dad saw Jimi Hendrix)	convenience store
	convenience store
art gallery	COLUMBIA
subsidized housing project	Pigeon Park Savings
COLUMBIA	empty lot
convenience store	convenience store
closed pawn shop	

subsidized housing project

United We Can
(poor people endeavouring every day
to make money by cleaning up your
environmentally friendly water bottles)

ginseng store

the Dodson

drop-in for the street

meth clinic

art gallery

CARRALL

Pigeon Park

pawn shop

closed business

the Beacon Hotel

Army and Navy

Vancouver Women's Health Collective

empty building

Funky Winkerbean's

city-sponsored Save-On-Meats

the Shaldon

meth clinic

subsidized housing project

closed business

the Only, closed due to the Health
Act (I never got sick eating there)

subsidized housing project

the Hotel Pennsylvania

CARRALL

Contemporary Centre for Asian Art

craft beer place

Pot Luck Café

a memory of tent city

a memory of tent city

a memory of tent city

a memory of tent city

the Grand Union

subsidized housing project

ABBOTT

the Paris Block

Acme Cafe

hooker store (Model Express)

parking lot

ABBOTT

SFU Woodward's

Goldcorp Centre for the Arts

store selling Chinese stuff

fancy furniture store

fancy furniture store

Bean Around the World

CAMBIE

closed pawn shop

convenience store

Salvation Army drop-in

retail space for lease

closed BeFresh Salon & Spa

fancy furniture store

Versus Training Center

Money Mart

discount fabric store

CAMBIE

superhooker in the hall of justice

in the city
i can be who i wanna
ain't no past tellin

i feel good today
and bam
i'm a stone cold fox
my ass is tight
and lookin right
i star in my own mtv videos
flashy cars, stacks a cash, fly hos
i'm makin boys run
ready to fire their gun

and tomorrow
i'm someone else

i got on my glasses, feelin smart
and bam
i'm deconstructing art
i'm eating lunch at a french cafe
talking about poetics over crème brulee
i'm gonna write books
about chinatown crooks
add to the story
tell all the glory

and tomorrow
i'm someone else

this city is feelin like rot
and i remember feeling caught
but today that don't make me feel like a tired ol ho
instead

i'm a cool motherfucker and i'm fully in control

and bam
i'm a superhero
i take this city by night
jumpin skyscrapers, midnight flight
i'm down for the fight
i give the ladies all my might
i show them cops wrong from right

i fly all over this city
a one woman committee
and i gather up all my girls
all my pearls

dead, almost, and alive

how it is (September 2012)

MAIN	MAIN
Owl Drugs	the heart of the community
no-name money mart	the Roosevelt
Hotel Washington	rest in peace AM & VS
convenience store	the Regent
empty building	dev. app. no. DE414810 approved
the Balmoral	dev. app. no. DE414810 approved
pizza shop	dev. app. no. DE414810approved
porn store	dev. app. no. DE414810 approved
Insite	dev. app. no. DE414810 approved
art gallery	the Brandiz
community garden	art gallery
empty building (the old Smilin' Buddha where my dad saw Jimi Hendrix)	convenience store
	convenience store
art gallery	COLUMBIA
subsidized housing project	Pigeon Park Savings
COLUMBIA	empty lot
convenience store	convenience store

closed pawn shop

the Shaldon

subsidized housing project

meth clinic

United We Can
(poor people endeavouring every day
to make money by cleaning up your
environmentally friendly water bottles)

subsidized housing project

closed business

the Only, closed due to the Health
Act (I never got sick eating there)

ginseng store

the Dodson

subsidized housing project

drop-in for the street

the Hotel Pennsylvania

meth clinic

Cartem's Donuts $27/dozen

art gallery

CARRALL

CARRALL

Contemporary Centre for Asian Art

Pigeon Park

craft beer place

pawn shop

Pot Luck Café

Window Community Art Shop

a memory of Olympic Tent Village

the Beacon Hotel

a memory of Olympic Tent Village

Army and Navy

a memory of Olympic Tent Village

Vancouver Women's Health
Collective

a memory of Olympic Tent Village

the Grand Union

empty building

subsidized housing project

Funky Winkerbean's

city-sponsored Save-On-Meats

the Paris Block

Acme Cafe

hooker store (Model Express)

parking lot

ABBOTT

SFU Woodward's

Goldcorp Centre for the Arts

store selling Chinese stuff

fancy furniture store

fancy furniture store

Bean Around the World

CAMBIE

ABBOTT

closed pawn shop

closed convenience store

closed Salvation Army drop-in

Work BC Employment Services

Au Soleil Salon & Spa

fancy furniture store

Versus Training Centre

Money Mart

discount fabric store

Vancouver Film School

CAMBIE

in dreams

the duress
the mess

it doesn't belong to the ladies and their people

instead

the duress
the fear

is yours

cause my arms are just that
strong and wide
these arms made of blood and bone
not pipelines not prisons not cops not judges
not ministries of what-the-fuck-ever
not residential schools not rezs
not truth and reconciliation industry

in my dreams

i slay you with my electric guitar
made of unceded wood
powered by woman blood and bone in earth
its sonic edge reverberates
through tailing lakes
resurrecting the birds
who take flight
an army of blackbirds
hunting you in the night

i kill the fascist within
whenever you

try murder
of this ground
and the people who own it

instead of you raping women in ancient trees
and me hearing their cries
you hear
my warrior cry
its sound so loud this earth shakes
the blood and bones in it recompose
they rally
they call war
and they win

the oil rigs me and my baby brother saw
as we drove all over Alberta
to visit our dad in correctional facilities
that span the same provinces as the pipelines
the institutions where you house the nation
i take them
extraction machineries
gathered in arms of blood and bone
up up up
the northern lights guide my way
and i hurl them
at all the prisons that held my dad
and made me ashamed
when people mistook this half yellow body for a red one

Matsqui, Mission, Mountain,
Drumheller, Bowden, BC Pen
prison industrial complex explodes
but all the right people live
and the blood and bones in this ground
is yours

i pick up a shard, pencil-sized
i write poems all over your pipelines
directing the oil back to the ground

in my dreams
i lay you motherfuckers down

how it is (November 2014)

MAIN

Owl Drugs

no-name money mart

Maple Hotel (PPP Canada SRO Initiative)

convenience store

empty building

the Balmoral

pizza shop

porn store

Insite

rest in peace Bud Osborn

art gallery

community garden

empty building (the old Smilin' Buddha
where my dad saw Jimi Hendrix)

art gallery

subsidized housing project

COLUMBIA

MAIN

the heart of the community

the Roosevelt

rest in peace AM & VS

the Regent

dev. app. no. DE414810 approved

79 units of market housing

9 units of "affordable" housing

9 units at welfare-shelter rate

dev. app. no. DE414810 approved

the Brandiz

art gallery

convenience store

convenience store

COLUMBIA

Pigeon Park Savings

empty lot

convenience store

convenience store

closed pawn shop

subsidized housing project

United We Can
closed and moved 2km out of the DTES

ginseng store

the Dodson

drop-in for the street

meth clinic

art gallery

CARRALL

Pigeon Park

closed pawn shop

closed business

the Beacon Hotel

Army and Navy

Vancouver Women's Health Collective

empty building

Funky Winkerbean's

the Shaldon

meth clinic

subsidized housing project

closed business

the Only, closed due to the Health Act
(I never got sick eating there)

subsidized housing project

the Hotel Pennsylvania

CARRALL

fancy lighting store

craft beer place

Pot Luck Café

100% social housing now!

100% social housing now!

100% social housing now!

100% social housing now!

the Grand Union

subsidized housing project

ABBOTT

city-sponsored Save-On-Meats

the Paris Block

Acme Cafe

hooker store (Model Express)

parking lot

ABBOTT

SFU Woodward's

Goldcorp Centre for the Arts

store selling Chinese stuff

fancy furniture store

fancy furniture store

Bean Around the World

CAMBIE

closed pawn shop

convenience store

Salvation Army drop-in

Work BC Employment Services

retail space for lease

closed BeFresh Salon & Spa

fancy furniture store

Versus Training Center

Money Mart

discount fabric store

Vancouver Film School

CAMBIE

post hooker micro.macro

i. unceded

I'll wage an insurrection
against/beside/from below
disavowing my connection

but as I climb
(yes, it's vertical here too)
the rhyme drops

like a yellow prairie son
a common man
a jerk

its good that it's not all about me anymore
but does it have to be so close to all about you

here
lyrical I battles I need to grow
cultivate aesthetic methodologies
in unseeded territory

it's a lie, this poem
it's not about you but it is

and in order for me to explain
I have to explain like you would
and I'm a lazy scholar
so I'll do it my way

you're white
and when you say
the acknowledgment
doesn't mean anything

you're wrong
or
you're correct
where you are
where I am sometimes

but you're honest
and you helped me arm myself for this
attached that tricky little clasp at the back of the maille protecting
my neck

but it's wider
this blood-soaked earth that makes my half-race step sticky
and it needs to be acknowledged
by me
and by you

ii. my affective labour

this can I come in/can I not
is an awful lot
like going out in glossy Gastown with my girl
not the waiting to see if we'll get in
cause shit, me and my girl don't wait
but easy entrance doesn't mean through the door

do I look good enough
tight
poetic
enough?
it seems like it should be different here because it's not about
looks/money/youth/money
and my hot to trot story was what got me across the
threshold

a plus here
a minus there
and sometimes you're super fresh
and then you just ain't
it's like that with sex work too
I wish I'd charged more for my first foray
into that space of trade

would you like to buy it
it's after-school-special good
turned myself out on my 23rd birthday
wearing the dress my grandma bought me

a burgundy babydoll
with a cheap rayon skirt
falling midway between knee and pussy
a bow at the back
tying me up like some sweet little birthday present for
someone

Charlie, I believe his name was
$80 for half and half in his little car
in some alley just off Clark and Venables

is it bad that I can't remember the exact alley?
should it be burned into my memory, just like my clean date?
I can't remember that shit either
now my body of intellectual work
is about
the work
I did
with my body

so I'm selling
with my body

how it is (July 2016)

MAIN	MAIN
Owl Drugs	the heart of the community
no-name money mart	renovating the Roosevelt to Molson Bank
Maple Hotel (PPP Canada SRO Initiative)	rest in peace AM & VS
convenience store	the Regent
empty building	Sequel 138
the Balmoral	Sequel 138
pizza shop	Sequel 138
porn store	Sequel 138
Insite	Sequel 138
rest in peace Bud Osborn	the Brandiz
boarded-up building	art gallery
community garden	closed convenience store
SBC Restaurant (the old Smilin' Buddha where my dad saw Jimi Hendrix)	convenience store
	COLUMBIA
building for sale	Pigeon Park Savings
subsidized housing project	empty lot
COLUMBIA	convenience store

convenience store

closed pawn shop

subsidized housing project

social mix housing

market/subsidized/social

the Dodson

drop-in for the street

meth clinic

art gallery

CARRALL

Pigeon Park

closed pawn shop

dev. app. no. DE418918

the Beacon Hotel

Army and Navy

Vancouver Women's Health Collective

empty building

Funky Winkerbean's

city-sponsored Save-On-Meats

the Shaldon

meth clinic

subsidized housing project

closed business

the Only, closed due to the Health Act
(I never got sick eating there)

subsidized housing project

the Hotel Pennsylvania

CARRALL

fancy lighting store

craft beer place

Pot Luck Café

Vancouver Tent City

Vancouver Tent City

Vancouver Tent City

Vancouver Tent City

the Grand Union

subsidized housing project

ABBOTT

the Paris Block

Acme Cafe

hooker store (Model Express)

parking lot

ABBOTT

SFU Woodward's

Goldcorp Centre for the Arts

retail and office space for lease

retail and office space for lease

Purebread

Bean Around the World

CAMBIE

coffee shop frequented
by skinny-jeans-wearers

$7 juice store

Salvation Army drop-in

Work BC Employment Services

retail space for lease

back to Au Soliel Salon & Spa

fancy furniture store

another fitness place

Money Mart

discount fabric store

Vancouver Film School

CAMBIE

weapons

i want aks and lugers and walther ppks
i want typewriters and barbed wire
i want panopticons and control over value
i wanna hurt people
i wanna cut them open
see how they work
i wanna buy them, own them
map
and
categorize
them

i wanna make them my object.
in a sentence, i act on them.

i have this tool belt see
it's powerful
i got it from you
and i know it works

its evidence is in my body, this mixed race body

you had your cartographers
and language
and ships
and taxonomy
and guns
and progress

but i got all that
plus i'm fucking fierce

and this time
it's me taking the women motherfuckers

but i wanna set free them
and own you

this time
i'm a pirate
and your pathetic white ass is my booty
this time
i lead the ship

this time
i'm at the helm
in nothin but panties
and a leather belt that holds my sword

does that fantasy work for you man?
a sexy bare-breasted halfbreed with dusky skin?

I steer the ship this time.

your navy tries to stop me
but i don't capitulate
like a white actress
playing a coloured woman
in the old movies
would

nah, i take my sword
the one you're supposed to turn on me
and
and I cut you with it

i make you and your sailors
give me and my all-woman marauding crew pedicures
while we storm the seas

you don't even see us comin

AFTERWORD

there goes the neighbourhood!

1)
I write this reflection in Spring 2016, on the occasion of the second printing *Mercenary English*, a book of poetry about the Downtown Eastside of Vancouver, just having made the decision to move out of the area. I've lived in the DTES since 1996, first at a rooming house in Chinatown, then an SRO on East Hastings, a major arterial road, then here, a studio apartment at 22 East Cordova Street that faces the alley between Cordova and Hastings; I've occupied this apartment for nineteen years and I've never lived anywhere longer than I've lived here. Historically, the DTES was a working-class neighbourhood that includes many of the city's historic and living communities of colour: Chinatown, Japantown, and Hogan's Alley, where a Black community lived, are all here. In the 1990s the DTES was pathologized through sensationalised media coverage of the many women who were murdered and disappeared from the neighbourhood.

I'm leaving because I'm saddened by what the area's become: an expensive enclave that has displaced some of the city's most vulnerable people. For years, United We Can, the recycling depot, was located across the alley from my building; it was moved, forcing the poor people who do our recycling to travel further to do their work. Last summer the building was demolished—suddenly, surreally, I could see Hastings from my window—and construction began for a new condo tower. The noise is a constant assault: jackhammers sound like machine guns, sledgehammers repeatedly hit rebar—it sounds like a war. It *is* a war, a war on the poor, and the weapon is real-estate development.

Not only is my move approaching, so too is my best friend's birthday. For the past few years her birthdays have been complicated. Although we used to frequent many of the new businesses in the DTES together, now I try not to go to these exclusory spaces and my attempts to consume more ethically cause tension between us. Two years ago her birthday was incredibly fraught because of the DTES restaurant pickets, organized by various low-income community members and allies to protest the proliferation of upscale restaurants, bars, boutiques and condos that are a result of gentrification. We live in the same building and with only an alley entrance separating us from the pickets, they were a constant presence for us. Knowing that for her birthday dinner she'd want to go to the newest restaurant to open at the time, which was being picketed in tandem with the first picket that had begun five months earlier, and hoping to preempt any discussion of it, I suggested another up-scale restaurant we'd been to many times before.

When I moved to the Downtown Eastside in 1996, I was an addict and street sex worker, and the space that one of the picketed restaurants occupies was a second-hand shop, then a pharmacy where I filled my methadone prescription when I went into recovery, and the space above it, now occupied by expensive private residences, was low-income housing. I've changed too: in socioeconomic class and attendant privilege, I now typify the new residents that have displaced the kind of resident I used to be. My life is far removed from that of the women I worked with. For one, I am among the living.

So I would not cross the picket lines. Given my previous patronage of places like these, my best friend now sees this decision as arbitrary.

2)
In 2007, I took a creative writing class at Simon Fraser University (SFU) and as I was concurrently working through my time as a sex worker, I was necessarily writing about the DTES. I sought to map the terrain, the deteriorating hotels where Vancouver's poor shelter in substandard housing, the overpriced "convenience" stores, the closed businesses, the empty lots—a place from which a hundred women have been murdered in a few decades. I titled the poem "how it is," not realizing it would be a living poem—that I'd be compelled to record *how it* is again and again because of gentrification, a word I hadn't yet learned. There are three new maps for this edition of *Mercenary English.*

After presenting my poem, the instructor asked if I'd seen Vancouver photo-conceptual artist Stan Douglas's *Every Building on 100 West Hastings,* a digital photograph of one of the same blocks I had mapped textually. I wasn't impressed. There are no people in it, none of the low-income people that populate the area. Denise Blake Oleksijczuk, a professor in the School for Contemporary Arts at SFU, describes it as "desolate" and suggests

> [t]his particular way of representing the street can be understood as an allusion to not only the violence and neglect that caused its precipitous decline—the no trespassing signs on the six boarded-up buildings at the middle of the block are indication of the contempt that property owners have for the poor and homeless—but also the tragic situation that has recently brought so much attention to the area.

The "tragic situation" she refers to is the missing and murdered women of the DTES. Citing feminist psychoanalyst Kaja Silverman's proposal that social relations can be transformed though a process of visual ideation, Oleksijczuk contends that the absent people, including the murdered and missing women, beg the question of where they are and allow viewers to engage in a process of visual ideation. I don't believe this process counters stereotypical media representations of the women as *drug-addicted prostitutes* with *high-risk lifestyles.* For some of us, this erasure is lived, not the subject (object?) of art. Some of us remember the police denying that a(nother) serial killer was murdering women from the neighbourhood, even though in only one year fourteen women were disappeared from this tiny area of the city.

3)
Is my decision not to cross the picket line arbitrary? My best friend says she doesn't understand why I'll go to ---, another of the new restaurants in the DTES, but not to the picketed ones. One, there's no picket, and two, the owner is an Asian woman, and an Asian woman opening a business in Chinatown makes sense to me. Maybe to my

best friend my decisions aren't arbitrary so much as hypocritical: I won't cross because people I know will see me, but at a place with no picket they won't. Here's how I worked it out a few years ago: I won't to go to any new place that opens in the neighbourhood, with much less frequency I'll go to places I've already patronized with her if I'm with her, and if I'm not with her, I won't. At times of course this breaks down, like when the NBA playoffs start and I'll go to ANY bar showing the game, like the sports bar in the new SFU Woodward's building.

In 1993, the long-standing Canadian department store chain Woodward's bankrupted and its store on East Hastings closed. Calls to use the vacant building for social housing were immediate, but it stood empty while low-income folks, many with physical and mental health issues, lacked housing. The Province bought the building then sold it to a developer on the condition that it provide social housing. While the police were publically denying that a serial killer was murdering women from the DTES, the developer told the provincial government that it couldn't mix social and market housing so the Province bought back the site in 2001. In September 2002, community members and allies set up Woodsquat, a tent city, around the perimeter of the building, occupying the sidewalk space for three months. In 2003, the City of Vancouver purchased the building from the Province, the same year the City secured the bid for the 2010 Olympics, the same year a preliminary hearing determined there was enough evidence to put Robert Pickton on trial for multiple murders of women from the DTES. After the City won the bid, slowly but steadily spaces of upscale consumption, then habitation, began to proliferate.

4)
The pickets were timed to occur during dinner hours and coincided with my work schedule so that I would return home, hungry and tired, to enter the pickets. Daily I stopped to say hello, feeling compelled to stay longer but not doing so, instead feeding and resting myself while others protested the fact that others do not have food to eat

or a place to rest. I felt guilty because I wanted to walk another way home to avoid the pickets.

5)
The central focus of the atrium at SFU Woodward's is Stan Douglas's *Abbott & Cordova, 7 August 1971*, a photographic mural on transparent glass; it depicts a protest at one of the intersections the building occupies, just a block north of the block he photographed in 2001 for *Every Building*. A real-estate development like SFU Woodward's is a powerful agent of gentrification, bringing together the university, the arts, retail, and private property, with a small number of social housing units insufficient to meet demand but included to meet the City's requirements. Why aestheticize a protest over the right to public space for the property-buying classes? Is it for the low-income residents too, who are segregated from the renters and owners of the market housing units by separate entrances and elevators? Every day Douglas's photograph looms over me as I bear witness to more and more low-income folks displaced by upwardly-mobile young folks who attend the art school and say things like: "this dance performance is inspired by the gestures of addicts in the DTES and is a feminist recontextualization of...." I love my best friend's remake of *Abbott & Cordova*. She's Photoshopped Snoop Dogg into the foreground, who's strolling east down Cordova with a Louis Vuitton bag over his arm while Godzilla approaches from the back left. At the centre of the image, the intersection, stands a gigantic bored and sleepy Persian kitten; she's like: why are you disturbing my nap with your hippie riot? I don't like the inclusion of the white male hipster leaning on his bike, but his presence is an accurate representation of the changes in the DTES in the time passed since the unveiling of Douglas's image just before the Olympics and my friend's remake a few years later. Every Building represents the architecture of the DTES before a wave of gentrification rolls through while *Abbott & Cordova* is part of the architecture of a building complex that anchored gentrification in DTES.

6)
This year for my best friend's—for my sister's—birthday, we're going to the newest place in Chinatown, opened by the aforementioned Asian restauranteur. We've already checked it out and I love it. I imagine places like it existed in the 50s and 60s back when my grandfather owned a Chinatown supper club and Chinatown was hopping at night. This year will be the first I will come to the DTES for her birthday rather than set out from it. This reflection on Mercenary English, written as I make a radical change in my life, is for the love of the many sisters, living or not, who I have shared this hood with and who have taught me so many things but above all, resiliency. I hope that it honours the little piece of unceded Coast Salish Territories I have lived on for the last twenty years.

echolocation: in conversation with Fred Moten

FRED MOTEN: So, by way of the afterword you wrote, "there goes the neighbourhood!", I wonder where neighbourhoods go. Where does the neighbourhood go? And then it's like how does the neighbourhood go in your poetry? Go, here, means live. How does the neighbourhood, this confluence of people and place, the place the people make in their living and in their collaborative and never individuated mattering, live/go (move) in your poetry?

MERCEDES ENG: I see the neighbourhood as the people, people who live in a particular place yes, and for some neighbourhood means location but to me a neighbourhood is the people in a specific geography that give that area its character. Now the neighbourhood (people) is being displaced by a new neighbourhood (people) occupying the physical space of the Downtown Eastside (DTES). How does the hood live in my poetry? "how it is," a poem now in its tenth year, continues to record the violence in the DTES caused by racism and real-estate development. I have a duty, also I think, a right, to bear witness and document.

FM: This connection between right and duty is cool and seems absolute to me and follows from that sense of the neighbourhood being the people, you and your women holding each other up, the hard and brutal but also beautiful life of the neighbourhood that is given so amazingly in the "autocartography" section of *Mercenary English*, which intersperses "how it is," which is like the neighbourhood's constantly changing map, with poems that feel not just autobiographical in the strictly personal sense but something like an autobiography of the neighbourhood as it goes and is made to go. Whenever you use the word "I" it's not just you and wherever you go the neighbourhood goes with you.

ME: This idea that the neighbourhood goes with me wherever I go reminded me of something I wrote about ten years ago, as I was theorizing my body as a space, as frontier, and as contact zone:

My body is the frontier and the contact zone. It's bruised, it's scarred. In a physical sense I seem not to know where my body ends and the rest of the world begins. At work as a waitress, it is as if I fight the barrier of class physically. I war while I work, as if banging into the tables of these lawyers I serve will create a bigger space for working class/female/ not white me. In another sense my body was a contact zone, a frontier, as a vehicle of sex work. My clients came to the frontier of poor spatiality in two ways. The male interloper enters the physical geography of the Downtown Eastside, Canada's poorest postal code, a space I'm allowed to be in because he needs me there to service him. Once the location becomes economically desirable, my space will disappear. Then he enters the physical geography, the body of the woman he rents, mine, which is not just what it is—a space to be neocolonized—because of where it is (the ghetto)—but also because her body, mine, is already written as a site of exploitation because it's female, because it's not white. Not that every girl on low track was not white. But so many of them were not. I no longer work the stroll. I don't stand at Dunlevy and Hastings til the early morning picking up dates outside the funeral parlour where my grandparents were shown, I don't pick up condoms and lube and the new bad date sheet as part of my routine anymore. But because it's my body, because it's where I live, I still carry the frontier, the contact zone, with me wherever I go.

FM: So the neighbourhood goes with you, as you are the neighbourhood. And if the neighbourhood is the displaced, rather than the scene of their displacement, then how and where does the neighbourhood go, or keep on going?

ME: I hadn't even thought of "goes" in "there goes the neighbourhood" as in where did the displaced low income people go to; I associate the phrase with white people voluntarily leaving because of black people and people of colour moving in, so from a propertied perspective, goes means devaluation in the form of decreasing property values.

Voiced by a person of colour who believes that safe and affordable housing is a right and fights for it, goes means devaluation in the form of decreasing low-income housing stock caused by increasing property values that correlate with an influx of upper middle class (often white) people to an area.

FM: But when they say there goes the neighbourhood, in spite of their own intentions, whether we are moving in or moving out, I always think they really mean there is the neighbourhood, there, there it goes, in those people. I don't think the occupiers ever actually have a neighbourhood. They are not our or one another's neighbours. I guess that's why I think the neighbourhood isn't occupied but displaced, made to move, by the ones who are both repulsed by it and attracted to it. And the next question, whether it is "how do we stop them," or "how do we move them" or "how do we kill them" or "how do we take what is them and theirs," is always, essentially, the same. This is what your book finds so many ways of showing!!! The neighbourhood goes with you, in your work and your words but also in the fact that even under the absolute duress of the settler, of which gentrification is just a new instantiation (or, more accurately, for which gentrification is a new name), the neighbourhood is a better way to live than the way of the occupiers. It's like they come to get what we have while also coming to kill it in this whole fucked-up economy in which genocide and accumulation never stop going together. I am interested in a critique of gentrification that proceeds from the assumption that we live better than them rather than they live better than us. (And I want you please to excuse my wanton use of the word we in the hope that there's a point up in it that justifies it, at least for a minute.) The neighbours live better than the occupiers (the settlers) even when the occupiers do all they can to make the lives of the neighbours unlivable.

ME: I'm fairly certain any "we" you're including yourself in is one I wanna be included in. A critique of gentrification that assumes "we live better than them rather than they live better than us" is compelling. I encountered a similar critique in Tings Chak's beautifully illustrated book on migrant detention in Canada, *Undocumented:*

The Architecture of Migrant Detention. Chak, an architect, multidisciplinary artist, and migrant justice organizer, writes that "in a securitized world, the gated community mirrors the detention centre, the micro-condominium isn't so different from the cell, they are sites of exclusion and seclusion" (30). Initially I thought: come on, now! Renting or owning a micro-condo is not the same as being incarcerated and living in a prison cell. But as I continue to think of the many people I know who have all the things they think they want, including property, but are still anxious, unhappy, and fiercely protective of their rights whenever a discussion of others' (lack of) rights surfaces, I'm beginning to shift my perception.

FM: Have you displaced yourself? What's the relation between this kind of self-displacement as modernist or postmodernist technique and what it is to be a kind of object of one's own gentrification, one's own improvement, where improvement, under the most severe duress, is another name for having survived, for having remained, as you say, among the living? Why is it that to remain among the living one has to leave? Where did the neighbourhood go in you, with you, if not, or if also, from you? And what's poetry got to do with all this downward and outward and upward mobility? Do down and out and up even properly signify? And how might poetry show that failure, while enacting another movement in the history of documenting and fostering nonpredatory movement?

ME: Have I displaced myself? Can I? I think of displacement as forced movement though I guess that's thinking narrowly. I feel like I have been forced by the negative psychic energy radiating from entitled people new to the area, by the continued and new violence against poor people. I don't know about self-displacement as modernist or postmodernist technique, only as a necessity: I felt so angry towards the new folks in the DTES and couldn't live like that anymore. What you say about a gentrification of self, my improvement of myself, is interesting but I find it difficult to think of gentrification as improvement. Kind of like the word revitalization that is often used to describe the processes of gentrification. But there is already life in the DTES, just not lives that are valued.

FM: "how it is" keeps moving in its documentation of people being moved, of people leaving. It is quick (living), not dead. It's different from the rest of "autocartography" because it feels like the self-displacement is more severe, or already has happened, so that a lot of that *expansive/displacing* lyric "I" is gone, replaced by an eye that sounds, music made from walking and noticing independent of subjective content or comment. What's it mean to say, I'm gone? There are no people in Douglas's *Every Building on 100 West Hastings*, as you say, but are there people in "how it is"? Where did everyone go? How does everyone go? And what if this is a question that isn't just about activating that Silverman project, some kind of recovery of the disappeared and their disappeared subjectivity? And what if it's not about countering stereotypes, either. What if the question of where and how they go is really a question about what it is to survive?

ME: Do the mapping poems say I'm gone? I don't know Douglas's intentions but in my work I'm most definitely trying to counter stereotypes. Do you think the absence of people in Douglas's *Every Building* asks the question of "what it is to survive"? I like his work and find it compelling though often I feel like I don't get it; over time I've come to understand that the lack of people in *Every Building* may not be an erasure, nor trying to activate the ideation thing, but my first reaction to *Every Building* was strong and it was: why aren't we here? My response to Douglas's work lacks scholarly criticality; it's informed by being a subject who did survive but is missing in his representation of the DTES and who now wants to throw a brick through *Abbott & Cordova, 7 August 1971*, his snazzy million $ glass installation at SFU Woodward's, to say: I'm still here! Except I'm not. Because I left the DTES. Because snazzy million $ glass installations are more important than low-income housing. A decade later, I feel differently about *Every Building*, but when I see it, part of me still yells: why aren't we here?

FM: It's like what you do in "how it is" that is analogous to *Every Building* (and there's that cool echo of Beckett in your title that parallels Douglas's deep interest in Beckett, too; and people remain in Beckett) is supplemented by the people, who are the ground of everything anyway. You ask why aren't we here and then you show where we are and where and how we go. A kind of southern US black vernacular thing is underlying all I have been saying. Like imagine the DTES was in Memphis or New Orleans. Then, instead of saying "I'm still here," in having thrown the brick through the window she might say, instead, "Here I go." This grammatical difference is in my head as I am thinking about that phrase and how it works in your stuff. And then, see, that horrible thing of "I'm still here" except that I'm not is what's there all the time in the formation, "there I go," or "there we go," or "t/here goes the neighbourhood." There it is; it's not there. So when I say all this is in my head when I am reading your work I mean to say that your work puts it there, lets it be there, in resonating with my own ways of seeing and talking. Your work is like a meeting place for the displaced. Your work is where we go for that. Your work is where we go. And to see *Every Building* differently and still to ask the question of why aren't we here—that speaks to something deep and important in Douglas's work, too. Maybe it's right to say he generates that question or maybe it's better to say he makes a place, or better yet, a way for it. And then, in asking that question, and in the wake of that asking, there goes Mercedes Eng saying here we are (not here); here we go, motherfucker!

ME: Oh, I love it, this interpretation of "go" in "there goes the neighbourhood"! I love it that my work says: Here we go, motherfucker! As we've been having this conversation, I've been listening to rapper ScHoolboy Q's new album, frequently interspersed with my favourite song ever of his, "There He Go," which speaks to this meaning of go— it's not only about going but also *how* he goes. And how does he go? As my favorite line declares: "chiefin like a motherfuckin Seminole."

FM: A practical question: do you worry about the poeticness or not of the word motherfucker? Does that word present formal problems?

ME: Like colonizers and capitalists, I wanna use language as a weapon and swearing and vernacular are some of the ways I weaponize English, so yeah I see a poeticness to the word motherfucker. I don't know about formal problems but I'm concerned about an appropriation (with all negative connotations that the word carries) of black vernacular. When I started listening to rap, I finally heard a language like my father's—a prison English full of cusses and slang—an English that embarrassed me when I was a kid. But now, for me, this language signifies a form of creative political resistance.

FM: Also: what happens when beauty breaks out in the documentation of genocide? I mean the trace of a singular rhythm that becomes yours in your having found it in Paul Strand's speech over and beyond or underneath and inside his genocidal spew. Abrasion and Flow between pages 36 and 37.

ME: Even though what I write about is dark, there's often humour, which I can see as a kind of a beauty in being able to document genocide honestly and also creatively through a kind of textual transgression that uses their own words against them. This is how my humour works in writing and in life. Last April the VPD shot and killed a black man in the DTES. I heard the shots then ran towards the sounds. A few days later, my partner commented that I hadn't been eating much and I joked that if the cops kept killing folks in the neighbourhood, I would be skinny for my summer trip to LA.

FM: Do you aestheticize? If so, why? What if "aestheticization" is where and how we go, keep going, keep moving, remain with the living in our leaving?

ME: Aestheticizing how it is is how I keep going. I aestheticize because poetry is one of my weapons against people who abuse their power.

FM: There's this famous poem by Countee Cullen that ends "yet Do I marvel at this curious thing / To make a poet black and bid him sing." A more curious and more marvelous and more terrible thing: to sing with a strange man's dick in your mouth or to speak, to come to voice through and to that man having known that, opening my mouth to shut it all the history of the blur between person and property is held in the blur between the mouth that sucks and the mouth that sings, that trembles concrete, the MRAD of the neighbourhood.

ME: Lots of stuff about mouths in "February 2010" as I was thinking through censorship of opposition to the Olympics. I was so young in 2010. I was literally younger and I hadn't yet finished school, gotten a job, or made any money, so my sense of myself was different then. But also, I hadn't so concretely put my body into the street for political reasons. Protesting the Olympics was when my beliefs became praxis, and I was ready, able, to oppose the violence of genocide and accumulation, which my whole life has been teaching me about, but it was during the Olympics that I voiced and bodied my opposition to it in a public way. The poem about the dick my mouth was initiated by the fear I had that the City, in their effort to limit dissent and thus control public perception about the Olympics (everyone's super into it!), wouldn't grant the Memorial March Committee a permit. Knowing that many women were gonna march anyway both excited and scared me. I thought: these women are so tough to not be scared of the police, or to be scared and do it regardless! And the police were stockpiling all these weapons like the MRAD and I was worried they'd use them. But the march was glorious! You straight up can't fuck with these women.

FM: What is it to be held down by your women? Is that like being moved? Is being held down where the neighbourhood goes?

ME: This makes me think of that architecture workshop you conducted in Vancouver last year. I asked whether a place like St. Michael's Indian Residential School, which was demolished in 2015, where so much genocide occurred, can be subverted or if it's too haunted. Your response (I'm paraphrasing) was that everywhere is haunted and that wherever you walk, you seek to be held by a maternal ecology. So now I'm thinking of being held down by my women as being cradled by a material ecology, their bones in the ground the foundation that supports me and my work. Is being held down by my women like being moved? Yes, emotionally moved and compelled to movement, to action. Is being held down where the neighbourhood goes? Yes!

Acknowledgements

These poems were written on unceded Coast Salish Territories.

To the women I try to be worthy to represent, I hope to honour you in the work I do.

Thanks to Andrea Actis, Annharte, Carmen Papalia, Cecily Nicholson, Christine LeClerc, Clint Burnham, Cynthia Dewi Oka, David Chariandy, David Jefferess, Emily Fedoruk, Fred Wah, Hari Alluri, Ivan Drury, Jake Kennedy, Jeff Derksen, Jen Currin, Jules Boykoff, Larissa Lai, Peter McDonald, Press Release, Reg Johanson, Roger Farr, Standard Ink & Copy, Steve Collis, and Wayde Compton, for making me feel like I counted when I needed it.

Special thanks to Fred Moten for fellowship.

Thanks to the editors of the following publications, where versions of these poems have appeared: "how it is" in *Memewar*, *Canada and Beyond*, *The Capilano Review*, and *The Revolving City: 51 Poems and the Stories Behind Them* (Anvil P), and "in my dreams" in *The Enpipe Line* (Creekstone P) and *Geist*.

"knuckle sandwich" uses the arguments of Yasmin Jiwani's "Mediations of Domination: Gendered Violence Within and Across Borders" and Michael Yellow Bird's "Cowboys and Indians: Toys of Genocide, Icons of Imperialism" as an apparatus for found text from news sources such as *The Vancouver Sun*, *The Province*, *The Globe and Mail*, CTV and CBC, and a full-page ad from a daily about hair products in the form of a news article on violence against women.